Greatest Homework Excuse Book EVER

Written and illustrated by fourth grade students of

Sycolin Creek Elementary School in Leesburg, Virginia

Scholastic Inc.
New York   Toronto   London   Auckland   Sydney   Mexico City   New Delhi   Hong Kong   Buenos Aires

ORIGINAL COVER

MEET THE AUTHORS

Top Row, left to right:
Roman Colón, Harrison Wise, Maya Smith, Mrs. VanderWijst, Sela Carrington,
Cameron Warter, Kaitlyn Nguyen, Melanie Faliskie

Bottom Row, left to right:
Emily Schechter, Annie Norris, Samantha Carver, Olivia Dinman

This book is dedicated to the Sycolin Creek Salamanders!

My stomach was churning,
my face was burning,
my homework was nowhere to be found...
OH NO! Where'd it go?

I looked in my bag,
I dumped EVERYTHING out;
"She's getting closer!"
I wanted to shout.

I looked in my desk—
everything was in place,
so I peeked in my lunchbox, just in case...

2.

All I found was a cookie, and an orange, too.
Where is my homework?
Oh, what to do!

I know that I did it;
it was in here last night!
If I don't find it,
it won't be a pretty sight!

I was shaking in my seat;
I trembled like a mouse.
Oh, where is my homework?
Maybe back at my house!

"Psst!" a voice whispered in my ear.
"Check it out, kid; you've got nothing to fear."
He took out a book; it looked pretty clever.
He said, "Take it! It's the
   Greatest Homework Excuse Book Ever!"

I flipped open the book
and scanned the page.
Which one would save me
from her horrible rage?

EXCUSE 1:

I hope this won't be too much of an issue,
but my little brother was sick and...

USED MY HOMEWORK AS A TISSUE!

EXCUSE 2:

My mom reached for some wrapping paper,
but grabbed my homework instead!
I hope you don't mind...

IT GOT MAILED TO MY UNCLE FRED!

EXCUSE 3:

My doctor said something just to me,
"You are allergic to homework!
You can't do it, you see!"

She gave me a note,
a pass just for me.
Once I read it,
I smiled with glee!

Cut and give to teacher

Please excuse him
from doing his work.
If he starts looking sick,
take him to Mrs. Klerc.
If he starts turning red,
he needs to go home to bed.
This student is allergic to homework.

From, Dr. Kirk

8

9

EXCUSE 4:

My sister was bored because of the rain,
and she used my homework as a paper airplane!
She didn't know any better,
and it flew straight into the

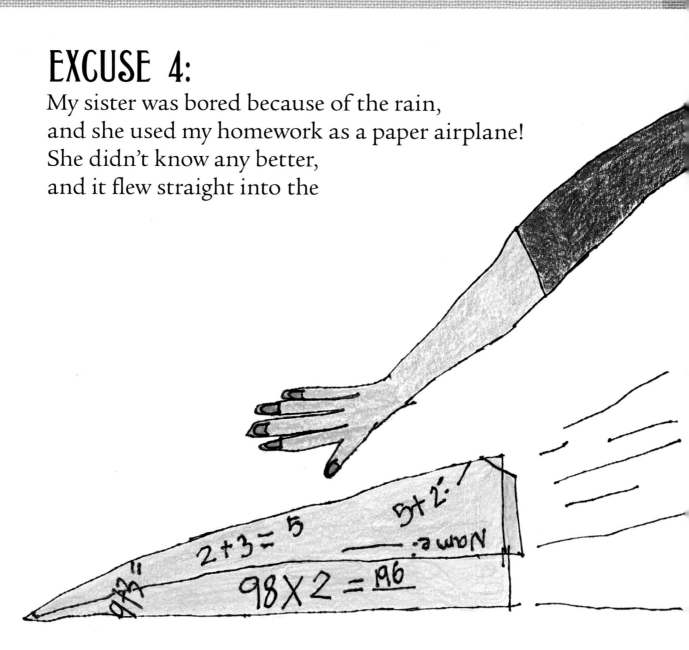

PAPER SHREDDER!

EXCUSE 5:

An alien kidnapped me last night;
it gave me a very, very big fright!

He wanted my homework
to power his ship.
I shouted and pouted
and puffed out my lip.
I cried out, "Oh BOO!"
but before I could save it,
he turned it to

GREEN GOO!

13

EXCUSE 6:

My sister was hungry,
but our cupboard was bare.
She picked up my homework;
she didn't care.

She rolled it up
and dipped it in milk,
then swallowed it down
like it was smooth as silk!

14

EXCUSE 7:

My mom grabbed my homework by mistake...

and baked it into the birthday cake!

EXCUSE 8:

My dog jumped on the counter,
looking for some bread.
To his surprise he found my homework
sitting there instead!

He gobbled it down with a chomp and a bite,
and stared up at me with a look of delight.

EXCUSE 9:

My sister was playing
   lacrosse,
and she used my homework
   to toss....
She always makes me cry!
Oh my! Oh my! Oh my!

EXCUSE 10:

I know you think of dog,
but this time it's a hog.
That pig, that juicy, juicy pig—
he used my homework as a wig!
Then he ate it in one swallow.
I guess his stomach was
hollow!

I closed the book and pondered my fate,
for which one of these excuses would she
take the bait?

My stomach was STILL churching,
my face was STILL burning,
my homework was STILL nowhere to be
found....

Should I blame it on my dog?
That's the classic for sure.
I just want this to be over...

I CAN'T TAKE IT ANYMORE!

20

2.1

Hmm? Should I tell the truth?
That's the best way to go.
At that moment I realized
the book was my foe.

This book of lies has got to go!
With a pitch and throw,
I chucked it out the window!

I looked my teacher straight in the eye.
Just like George Washington,
I cannot tell a lie.
"Last night I studied for the quiz,
but now I don't know where it is!"

She stopped in her tracks and
looked me straight in the eye.

"I'm SO happy you didn't tell me a lie!
Thanks for not giving me a silly excuse.
Kids ALWAYS do that;
It's really no use!

Just bring it tomorrow;
it's okay if it's overdue,
When I was little,
I did that once, too!"

I looked out the window and to my surprise,
another kid had picked up the book of lies!

He flipped through it with a smile of glee,
But that's another story; just wait and see!!!

Write and draw your Homework Excuse here:

Write and draw your Homework Excuse here:

Kids Are Authors®
Books written by children for children

The Kids Are Authors® Competition was established in 1986 to encourage
children to read and to become involved in the creative process of writing.

Since then, thousands of children have written and illustrated books as participants
in the Kids Are Authors® Competition.

The winning books in the annual competition are published by Scholastic Inc.
and are distributed by Scholastic Book Fairs throughout the United States.

For more information:
Kids Are Authors® 1080 Greenwood Blvd., Lake Mary, FL 32746
Or visit our web site at: www.scholastic.com/kidsareauthors

ISBN-10 0-545-21329-0

ISBN-13 978-0-545-21329-5

12 11 10 9 8 7 6 5 4 3 2 1

Cover and Design by Bill Henderson

Printed and bound in the U.S.A.
First Printing, July 2009